Planners & Stationery
by Sellers Publishing, Inc.

17-Month Weekly Planner
August 2023 ~ December 2024

featuring

jess phoenix

Name _____

Phone _____

Email _____

Astronomical information is in Eastern Time and Daylight Saving Time.
Key to abbreviations: United States (US), Canada (CAN), United Kingdom (UK),
Australia (AUS), South Australia (SA), Western Australia (W. Australia), Australian Capital Territory (ACT),
New Zealand (NZ), New South Wales (NSW), Queensland (QLD)

Goal Planning

████ TO CALL / EMAIL ████   ████ TO PURCHASE ████

_____   _____
_____   _____
_____   _____
_____   _____
_____   _____
_____   _____
_____   _____
_____   _____
_____   _____

GOAL   STEPS   DUE

☐ _____   _____
☐ _____   _____
☐ _____   _____
☐ _____   _____

GOAL   STEPS   DUE

☐ _____   _____
☐ _____   _____
☐ _____   _____
☐ _____   _____

GOAL   STEPS   DUE

☐ _____   _____
☐ _____   _____
☐ _____   _____
☐ _____   _____

 *To Do*

MUST DO

- [ ]
- [ ]
- [ ]
- [ ]
- [ ]
- [ ]
- [ ]

HOPE TO DO

- [ ]
- [ ]
- [ ]
- [ ]
- [ ]
- [ ]
- [ ]

NOTE TO SELF

Goal Planning

TO CALL / EMAIL

TO PURCHASE

_____ _____
_____ _____
_____ _____
_____ _____
_____ _____
_____ _____
_____ _____
_____ _____

GOAL　　　STEPS　　　　　　　　　　　　　　DUE

☐ _____ _____
☐ _____ _____
☐ _____ _____
☐ _____ _____

GOAL　　　STEPS　　　　　　　　　　　　　　DUE

☐ _____ _____
☐ _____ _____
☐ _____ _____
☐ _____ _____

GOAL　　　STEPS　　　　　　　　　　　　　　DUE

☐ _____ _____
☐ _____ _____
☐ _____ _____
☐ _____ _____

 To Do

MUST DO

- [ ]
- [ ]
- [ ]
- [ ]
- [ ]
- [ ]
- [ ]

HOPE TO DO

- [ ]
- [ ]
- [ ]
- [ ]
- [ ]
- [ ]
- [ ]

NOTE TO SELF

Goal Planning

TO CALL / EMAIL	TO PURCHASE
_____	_____
_____	_____
_____	_____
_____	_____
_____	_____
_____	_____
_____	_____

GOAL

STEPS	DUE
☐ _____	_____
☐ _____	_____
☐ _____	_____
☐ _____	_____

GOAL

STEPS	DUE
☐ _____	_____
☐ _____	_____
☐ _____	_____
☐ _____	_____

GOAL

STEPS	DUE
☐ _____	_____
☐ _____	_____
☐ _____	_____
☐ _____	_____

To Do

MUST DO

- [ ]
- [ ]
- [ ]
- [ ]
- [ ]
- [ ]
- [ ]

HOPE TO DO

- [ ]
- [ ]
- [ ]
- [ ]
- [ ]
- [ ]
- [ ]

NOTE TO SELF

Goal Planning

TO CALL / EMAIL

_____
_____
_____
_____
_____
_____
_____
_____

TO PURCHASE

_____
_____
_____
_____
_____
_____
_____
_____

GOAL

STEPS | DUE
- ☐ _____ _____
- ☐ _____ _____
- ☐ _____ _____
- ☐ _____ _____

GOAL

STEPS | DUE
- ☐ _____ _____
- ☐ _____ _____
- ☐ _____ _____
- ☐ _____ _____

GOAL

STEPS | DUE
- ☐ _____ _____
- ☐ _____ _____
- ☐ _____ _____
- ☐ _____ _____

 *To Do*

MUST DO

☐
☐
☐
☐
☐
☐
☐

HOPE TO DO

☐
☐
☐
☐
☐
☐
☐

NOTE TO SELF

Goal Planning

TO CALL / EMAIL	TO PURCHASE
_____	_____
_____	_____
_____	_____
_____	_____
_____	_____
_____	_____
_____	_____
_____	_____

GOAL   STEPS   DUE

☐ _____ _____
☐ _____ _____
☐ _____ _____
☐ _____ _____

GOAL   STEPS   DUE

☐ _____ _____
☐ _____ _____
☐ _____ _____
☐ _____ _____

GOAL   STEPS   DUE

☐ _____ _____
☐ _____ _____
☐ _____ _____
☐ _____ _____

 *To Do*

MUST DO

- ☐
- ☐
- ☐
- ☐
- ☐
- ☐
- ☐

HOPE TO DO

- ☐
- ☐
- ☐
- ☐
- ☐
- ☐
- ☐

NOTE TO SELF

Goal Planning

TO CALL / EMAIL	TO PURCHASE
_____	_____
_____	_____
_____	_____
_____	_____
_____	_____
_____	_____
_____	_____

GOAL

STEPS   DUE

☐ _____   _____

☐ _____   _____

☐ _____   _____

☐ _____   _____

GOAL

STEPS   DUE

☐ _____   _____

☐ _____   _____

☐ _____   _____

☐ _____   _____

GOAL

STEPS   DUE

☐ _____   _____

☐ _____   _____

☐ _____   _____

☐ _____   _____

To Do

MUST DO

- [ ]
- [ ]
- [ ]
- [ ]
- [ ]
- [ ]
- [ ]

HOPE TO DO

- [ ]
- [ ]
- [ ]
- [ ]
- [ ]
- [ ]
- [ ]

NOTE TO SELF

 August

SUNDAY	MONDAY	TUESDAY	WEDNESDAY
30	31	1 ○ Full Moon	2
6	7 Bank Holiday (NSW) Civic Holiday (Canada)	8	9
13	14	15	16 ● New Moon
20	21	22	23
27	28 Bank Holiday (UK)	29	30 ○ Full Moon

 *2023*

THURSDAY	FRIDAY	SATURDAY	NOTES
3	4	5	
10	11	12	
17	18	19	
24	25	26	
31	1	2	

JULY

S	M	T	W	T	F	S
						1
2	3	4	5	6	7	8
9	10	11	12	13	14	15
16	17	18	19	20	21	22
23	24	25	26	27	28	29
30	31					

SEPTEMBER

S	M	T	W	T	F	S
					1	2
3	4	5	6	7	8	9
10	11	12	13	14	15	16
17	18	19	20	21	22	23
24	25	26	27	28	29	30

July 2023

31 Monday

- [ ]
- [ ]
- [ ]
- [ ]
- [ ]
- [ ]

1 Tuesday   O Full Moon

- [ ]
- [ ]
- [ ]
- [ ]
- [ ]
- [ ]

2 Wednesday

- [ ]
- [ ]
- [ ]
- [ ]
- [ ]
- [ ]

August

AUGUST
S	M	T	W	T	F	S
		1	2	3	4	5
6	7	8	9	10	11	12
13	14	15	16	17	18	19
20	21	22	23	24	25	26
27	28	29	30	31		

3 Thursday

- [ ]
- [ ]
- [ ]
- [ ]
- [ ]
- [ ]

4 Friday

- [ ]
- [ ]
- [ ]
- [ ]
- [ ]
- [ ]

5 Saturday

- [ ]
- [ ]
- [ ]
- [ ]
- [ ]
- [ ]

6 Sunday

- [ ]
- [ ]
- [ ]
- [ ]
- [ ]
- [ ]

August 2023

7 Monday

- [ ]
- [ ]
- [ ]
- [ ]
- [ ]
- [ ]

8 Tuesday

- [ ]
- [ ]
- [ ]
- [ ]
- [ ]
- [ ]

9 Wednesday

- [ ]
- [ ]
- [ ]
- [ ]
- [ ]
- [ ]

AUGUST

S	M	T	W	T	F	S
		1	2	3	4	5
6	7	8	9	10	11	12
13	14	15	16	17	18	19
20	21	22	23	24	25	26
27	28	29	30	31		

10 Thursday

- [ ]
- [ ]
- [ ]
- [ ]
- [ ]
- [ ]

11 Friday

- [ ]
- [ ]
- [ ]
- [ ]
- [ ]
- [ ]

12 Saturday

- [ ]
- [ ]
- [ ]
- [ ]
- [ ]
- [ ]

13 Sunday

- [ ]
- [ ]
- [ ]
- [ ]
- [ ]
- [ ]

August 2023

14 Monday

15 Tuesday

16 Wednesday ● New Moon

AUGUST

S	M	T	W	T	F	S
		1	2	3	4	5
6	7	8	9	10	11	12
13	14	15	16	17	18	19
20	21	22	23	24	25	26
27	28	29	30	31		

17 Thursday

- [ ]
- [ ]
- [ ]
- [ ]
- [ ]
- [ ]

18 Friday

- [ ]
- [ ]
- [ ]
- [ ]
- [ ]
- [ ]

19 Saturday

- [ ]
- [ ]
- [ ]
- [ ]
- [ ]
- [ ]

20 Sunday

- [ ]
- [ ]
- [ ]
- [ ]
- [ ]
- [ ]

August 2023

21 Monday

- [ ]
- [ ]
- [ ]
- [ ]
- [ ]
- [ ]

22 Tuesday

- [ ]
- [ ]
- [ ]
- [ ]
- [ ]
- [ ]

23 Wednesday

- [ ]
- [ ]
- [ ]
- [ ]
- [ ]
- [ ]

AUGUST

S	M	T	W	T	F	S
		1	2	3	4	5
6	7	8	9	10	11	12
13	14	15	16	17	18	19
20	21	22	23	24	25	26
27	28	29	30	31		

24 Thursday

25 Friday

26 Saturday

27 Sunday

August 2023

28 Monday   Bank Holiday (UK)

- [ ]
- [ ]
- [ ]
- [ ]
- [ ]
- [ ]

29 Tuesday

- [ ]
- [ ]
- [ ]
- [ ]
- [ ]
- [ ]

30 Wednesday   ○ Full Moon

- [ ]
- [ ]
- [ ]
- [ ]
- [ ]
- [ ]

September

SEPTEMBER

S	M	T	W	T	F	S
					1	2
3	4	5	6	7	8	9
10	11	12	13	14	15	16
17	18	19	20	21	22	23
24	25	26	27	28	29	30

31 Thursday

- [ ]
- [ ]
- [ ]
- [ ]
- [ ]
- [ ]

1 Friday

- [ ]
- [ ]
- [ ]
- [ ]
- [ ]
- [ ]

2 Saturday

- [ ]
- [ ]
- [ ]
- [ ]
- [ ]
- [ ]

3 Sunday

Father's Day
(Australia, NZ)

- [ ]
- [ ]
- [ ]
- [ ]
- [ ]
- [ ]

September

SUNDAY	MONDAY	TUESDAY	WEDNESDAY
27	28	29	30
3 Father's Day (Australia, NZ)	4 Labor Day (US, Canada)	5	6
10	11 Patriot Day	12	13
17	18	19	20
24 Yom Kippur begins at sundown	25 King's Birthday (W. Australia)	26	27

 2023

THURSDAY	FRIDAY	SATURDAY	NOTES
31	1	2	
7	8	9	
14	15	16	
21 ● New Moon	22 Rosh Hashanah begins at sundown	23	
28 UN International Day of Peace	29	30 Autumnal Equinox	
	○ Full Moon		

AUGUST

S	M	T	W	T	F	S
		1	2	3	4	5
6	7	8	9	10	11	12
13	14	15	16	17	18	19
20	21	22	23	24	25	26
27	28	29	30	31		

OCTOBER

S	M	T	W	T	F	S
1	2	3	4	5	6	7
8	9	10	11	12	13	14
15	16	17	18	19	20	21
22	23	24	25	26	27	28
29	30	31				

September 2023

4 Monday
Labor Day (US, Canada)

- [ ]
- [ ]
- [ ]
- [ ]
- [ ]
- [ ]

5 Tuesday

- [ ]
- [ ]
- [ ]
- [ ]
- [ ]
- [ ]

6 Wednesday

- [ ]
- [ ]
- [ ]
- [ ]
- [ ]
- [ ]

SEPTEMBER

S	M	T	W	T	F	S
					1	2
3	4	5	6	7	8	9
10	11	12	13	14	15	16
17	18	19	20	21	22	23
24	25	26	27	28	29	30

7 Thursday

- [ ]
- [ ]
- [ ]
- [ ]
- [ ]
- [ ]

8 Friday

- [ ]
- [ ]
- [ ]
- [ ]
- [ ]
- [ ]

9 Saturday

- [ ]
- [ ]
- [ ]
- [ ]
- [ ]
- [ ]

10 Sunday

- [ ]
- [ ]
- [ ]
- [ ]
- [ ]
- [ ]

September 2023

11 Monday   Patriot Day

- [ ]
- [ ]
- [ ]
- [ ]
- [ ]
- [ ]

12 Tuesday

- [ ]
- [ ]
- [ ]
- [ ]
- [ ]
- [ ]

13 Wednesday

- [ ]
- [ ]
- [ ]
- [ ]
- [ ]
- [ ]

SEPTEMBER

S	M	T	W	T	F	S
					1	2
3	4	5	6	7	8	9
10	11	12	13	14	15	16
17	18	19	20	21	22	23
24	25	26	27	28	29	30

14 Thursday

● New Moon

- [ ]
- [ ]
- [ ]
- [ ]
- [ ]
- [ ]

15 Friday

Rosh Hashanah begins at sundown

- [ ]
- [ ]
- [ ]
- [ ]
- [ ]
- [ ]

16 Saturday

- [ ]
- [ ]
- [ ]
- [ ]
- [ ]
- [ ]

17 Sunday

- [ ]
- [ ]
- [ ]
- [ ]
- [ ]

September 2023

18 Monday

- [ ]
- [ ]
- [ ]
- [ ]
- [ ]
- [ ]

19 Tuesday

- [ ]
- [ ]
- [ ]
- [ ]
- [ ]
- [ ]

20 Wednesday

- [ ]
- [ ]
- [ ]
- [ ]
- [ ]
- [ ]

SEPTEMBER

S	M	T	W	T	F	S
					1	2
3	4	5	6	7	8	9
10	11	12	13	14	15	16
17	18	19	20	21	22	23
24	25	26	27	28	29	30

21 Thursday

UN International Day of Peace

- [ ]
- [ ]
- [ ]
- [ ]
- [ ]
- [ ]

22 Friday

- [ ]
- [ ]
- [ ]
- [ ]
- [ ]
- [ ]

23 Saturday

Autumnal Equinox

- [ ]
- [ ]
- [ ]
- [ ]
- [ ]
- [ ]

24 Sunday

Yom Kippur
begins at sundown

- [ ]
- [ ]
- [ ]
- [ ]
- [ ]
- [ ]

September 2023

25 Monday
King's Birthday (W. Australia)

26 Tuesday

27 Wednesday

October

OCTOBER

S	M	T	W	T	F	S
1	2	3	4	5	6	7
8	9	10	11	12	13	14
15	16	17	18	19	20	21
22	23	24	25	26	27	28
29	30	31				

28 Thursday

- [ ]
- [ ]
- [ ]
- [ ]
- [ ]
- [ ]

29 Friday

○ Full Moon

- [ ]
- [ ]
- [ ]
- [ ]
- [ ]
- [ ]

30 Saturday

- [ ]
- [ ]
- [ ]
- [ ]
- [ ]
- [ ]

1 Sunday

- [ ]
- [ ]
- [ ]
- [ ]
- [ ]
- [ ]

October

SUNDAY	MONDAY	TUESDAY	WEDNESDAY
1	2	3	4
	Labour Day (ACT, NSW, SA) King's Birthday (Queensland)		
8	9	10	11
	Indigenous Peoples' Day (observed) Columbus Day (observed) Thanksgiving (Canada)		
15	16	17	18
22	23	24	25
	Labour Day (New Zealand)		
29	30	31	1
		Halloween	

2023

THURSDAY	FRIDAY	SATURDAY	NOTES
5	6	7	
12	13	14 ● New Moon	
19	20	21	
26	27	28 ○ Full Moon	
2	3	4	

SEPTEMBER

S	M	T	W	T	F	S
					1	2
3	4	5	6	7	8	9
10	11	12	13	14	15	16
17	18	19	20	21	22	23
24	25	26	27	28	29	30

NOVEMBER

S	M	T	W	T	F	S
			1	2	3	4
5	6	7	8	9	10	11
12	13	14	15	16	17	18
19	20	21	22	23	24	25
26	27	28	29	30		

October 2023

Labour Day (ACT, NSW, SA)
King's Birthday (Queensland)

2 Monday

- [ ]
- [ ]
- [ ]
- [ ]
- [ ]
- [ ]

3 Tuesday

- [ ]
- [ ]
- [ ]
- [ ]
- [ ]
- [ ]

4 Wednesday

- [ ]
- [ ]
- [ ]
- [ ]
- [ ]
- [ ]

OCTOBER

S	M	T	W	T	F	S
1	2	3	4	5	6	7
8	9	10	11	12	13	14
15	16	17	18	19	20	21
22	23	24	25	26	27	28
29	30	31				

5 Thursday

- [ ]
- [ ]
- [ ]
- [ ]
- [ ]
- [ ]

6 Friday

- [ ]
- [ ]
- [ ]
- [ ]
- [ ]
- [ ]

7 Saturday

- [ ]
- [ ]
- [ ]
- [ ]
- [ ]
- [ ]

8 Sunday

- [ ]
- [ ]
- [ ]
- [ ]
- [ ]
- [ ]

October 2023

9 Monday

Indigenous Peoples' Day (observed)
Columbus Day (observed)
Thanksgiving (Canada)

☐
☐
☐
☐
☐
☐

10 Tuesday

☐
☐
☐
☐
☐
☐

11 Wednesday

☐
☐
☐
☐
☐
☐

OCTOBER

S	M	T	W	T	F	S
1	2	3	4	5	6	7
8	9	10	11	12	13	14
15	16	17	18	19	20	21
22	23	24	25	26	27	28
29	30	31				

12 Thursday

☐
☐
☐
☐
☐
☐

13 Friday

☐
☐
☐
☐
☐
☐

14 Saturday ● New Moon

☐
☐
☐
☐
☐
☐

15 Sunday

☐
☐
☐
☐
☐
☐

October 2023

16 Monday

- [ ]
- [ ]
- [ ]
- [ ]
- [ ]
- [ ]

17 Tuesday

- [ ]
- [ ]
- [ ]
- [ ]
- [ ]
- [ ]

18 Wednesday

- [ ]
- [ ]
- [ ]
- [ ]
- [ ]
- [ ]

OCTOBER

S	M	T	W	T	F	S
1	2	3	4	5	6	7
8	9	10	11	12	13	14
15	16	17	18	19	20	21
22	23	24	25	26	27	28
29	30	31				

19 Thursday

20 Friday

21 Saturday

22 Sunday

October 2023

23 Monday

Labour Day (New Zealand)

- [ ]
- [ ]
- [ ]
- [ ]
- [ ]
- [ ]

24 Tuesday

- [ ]
- [ ]
- [ ]
- [ ]
- [ ]
- [ ]

25 Wednesday

- [ ]
- [ ]
- [ ]
- [ ]
- [ ]
- [ ]

OCTOBER

S	M	T	W	T	F	S
1	2	3	4	5	6	7
8	9	10	11	12	13	14
15	16	17	18	19	20	21
22	23	24	25	26	27	28
29	30	31				

26 Thursday

☐
☐
☐
☐
☐
☐

27 Friday

☐
☐
☐
☐
☐
☐

28 Saturday   ○ Full Moon

☐
☐
☐
☐
☐
☐

29 Sunday

☐
☐
☐
☐
☐
☐

 November

SUNDAY	MONDAY	TUESDAY	WEDNESDAY
29	30	31	1 All Saints' Day
5 Daylight Saving ends	6	7 Election Day	8
12 Remembrance Sunday (UK)	13 ● New Moon	14	15
19	20	21	22
26	27 ○ Full Moon	28	29

2023

THURSDAY	FRIDAY	SATURDAY	NOTES
2	3	4	
9	10	11 Veterans Day Remembrance Day (CAN, AUS, NZ)	
16	17	18	
23 Thanksgiving	24	25	
30	1	2	

October 2023

30 Monday

- [ ]
- [ ]
- [ ]
- [ ]
- [ ]
- [ ]

31 Tuesday

Halloween

- [ ]
- [ ]
- [ ]
- [ ]
- [ ]
- [ ]

1 Wednesday

All Saints' Day

- [ ]
- [ ]
- [ ]
- [ ]
- [ ]
- [ ]

November

NOVEMBER

S	M	T	W	T	F	S
			1	2	3	4
5	6	7	8	9	10	11
12	13	14	15	16	17	18
19	20	21	22	23	24	25
26	27	28	29	30		

2 Thursday

- [ ]
- [ ]
- [ ]
- [ ]
- [ ]
- [ ]

3 Friday

- [ ]
- [ ]
- [ ]
- [ ]
- [ ]
- [ ]

4 Saturday

- [ ]
- [ ]
- [ ]
- [ ]
- [ ]
- [ ]

5 Sunday   Daylight Saving ends

- [ ]
- [ ]
- [ ]
- [ ]
- [ ]
- [ ]

November 2023

6 Monday

☐
☐
☐
☐
☐
☐

7 Tuesday   Election Day

☐
☐
☐
☐
☐
☐

8 Wednesday

☐
☐
☐
☐
☐
☐

NOVEMBER

S	M	T	W	T	F	S
			1	2	3	4
5	6	7	8	9	10	11
12	13	14	15	16	17	18
19	20	21	22	23	24	25
26	27	28	29	30		

9 Thursday

☐
☐
☐
☐
☐
☐

10 Friday

☐
☐
☐
☐
☐
☐

Veterans Day

11 Saturday

Remembrance Day
(CAN, AUS, NZ)

☐
☐
☐
☐
☐
☐

12 Sunday

Remembrance Sunday
(UK)

☐
☐
☐
☐
☐
☐

November 2023

13 Monday
●New Moon

☐
☐
☐
☐
☐
☐

14 Tuesday

☐
☐
☐
☐
☐
☐

15 Wednesday

☐
☐
☐
☐
☐
☐

NOVEMBER

S	M	T	W	T	F	S
			1	2	3	4
5	6	7	8	9	10	11
12	13	14	15	16	17	18
19	20	21	22	23	24	25
26	27	28	29	30		

16 Thursday

- [ ]
- [ ]
- [ ]
- [ ]
- [ ]
- [ ]

17 Friday

- [ ]
- [ ]
- [ ]
- [ ]
- [ ]
- [ ]

18 Saturday

- [ ]
- [ ]
- [ ]
- [ ]
- [ ]
- [ ]

19 Sunday

- [ ]
- [ ]
- [ ]
- [ ]
- [ ]
- [ ]

November 2023

20 Monday

☐
☐
☐
☐
☐
☐

21 Tuesday

☐
☐
☐
☐
☐
☐

22 Wednesday

☐
☐
☐
☐
☐
☐

NOVEMBER

S	M	T	W	T	F	S
			1	2	3	4
5	6	7	8	9	10	11
12	13	14	15	16	17	18
19	20	21	22	23	24	25
26	27	28	29	30		

23 Thursday

Thanksgiving

24 Friday

25 Saturday

26 Sunday

November 2023

27 Monday
○ Full Moon

- [ ]
- [ ]
- [ ]
- [ ]
- [ ]
- [ ]

28 Tuesday

- [ ]
- [ ]
- [ ]
- [ ]
- [ ]
- [ ]

29 Wednesday

- [ ]
- [ ]
- [ ]
- [ ]
- [ ]
- [ ]

December

DECEMBER
S	M	T	W	T	F	S
					1	2
3	4	5	6	7	8	9
10	11	12	13	14	15	16
17	18	19	20	21	22	23
24	25	26	27	28	29	30
31						

30 Thursday

- [ ]
- [ ]
- [ ]
- [ ]
- [ ]
- [ ]

1 Friday

- [ ]
- [ ]
- [ ]
- [ ]
- [ ]
- [ ]

2 Saturday

- [ ]
- [ ]
- [ ]
- [ ]
- [ ]
- [ ]

3 Sunday

- [ ]
- [ ]
- [ ]
- [ ]
- [ ]
- [ ]

 December

SUNDAY	MONDAY	TUESDAY	WEDNESDAY
26	27	28	29
3	4	5	6
10	11	12 ● New Moon	13
17	18	19	20
24/31	25 Christmas	26 Boxing Day (CAN, UK, AUS, NZ) Kwanzaa begins ○ Full Moon	27

 2023

THURSDAY	FRIDAY	SATURDAY	NOTES
30	1	2	
7	8	9	
	Pearl Harbor Remembrance Day		
	Hanukkah begins at sundown		
14	15	16	
21	22	23	
Winter Solstice			
28	29	30	

NOVEMBER

S	M	T	W	T	F	S
			1	2	3	4
5	6	7	8	9	10	11
12	13	14	15	16	17	18
19	20	21	22	23	24	25
26	27	28	29	30		

JANUARY 2024

S	M	T	W	T	F	S
	1	2	3	4	5	6
7	8	9	10	11	12	13
14	15	16	17	18	19	20
21	22	23	24	25	26	27
28	29	30	31			

December 2023

4 Monday

- [ ]
- [ ]
- [ ]
- [ ]
- [ ]
- [ ]

5 Tuesday

- [ ]
- [ ]
- [ ]
- [ ]
- [ ]
- [ ]

6 Wednesday

- [ ]
- [ ]
- [ ]
- [ ]
- [ ]
- [ ]

DECEMBER
S	M	T	W	T	F	S
					1	2
3	4	5	6	7	8	9
10	11	12	13	14	15	16
17	18	19	20	21	22	23
24	25	26	27	28	29	30
31						

7 Thursday

Pearl Harbor
Remembrance Day

☐   Hanukkah begins at sundown

☐

☐

☐

☐

☐

8 Friday

☐

☐

☐

☐

☐

☐

9 Saturday

☐

☐

☐

☐

☐

☐

10 Sunday

☐

☐

☐

☐

☐

☐

December 2023

11 Monday

☐
☐
☐
☐
☐
☐

12 Tuesday
● New Moon

☐
☐
☐
☐
☐
☐

13 Wednesday

☐
☐
☐
☐
☐
☐

DECEMBER

S	M	T	W	T	F	S
					1	2
3	4	5	6	7	8	9
10	11	12	13	14	15	16
17	18	19	20	21	22	23
24	25	26	27	28	29	30
31						

14 Thursday

- [ ]
- [ ]
- [ ]
- [ ]
- [ ]
- [ ]

15 Friday

- [ ]
- [ ]
- [ ]
- [ ]
- [ ]
- [ ]

16 Saturday

- [ ]
- [ ]
- [ ]
- [ ]
- [ ]
- [ ]

17 Sunday

- [ ]
- [ ]
- [ ]
- [ ]
- [ ]
- [ ]

December 2023

18 Monday

19 Tuesday

20 Wednesday

DECEMBER

S	M	T	W	T	F	S
					1	2
3	4	5	6	7	8	9
10	11	12	13	14	15	16
17	18	19	20	21	22	23
24	25	26	27	28	29	30
31						

21 Thursday

Winter Solstice

- [ ]
- [ ]
- [ ]
- [ ]
- [ ]
- [ ]

22 Friday

- [ ]
- [ ]
- [ ]
- [ ]
- [ ]
- [ ]

23 Saturday

- [ ]
- [ ]
- [ ]
- [ ]
- [ ]
- [ ]

24 Sunday

- [ ]
- [ ]
- [ ]
- [ ]
- [ ]
- [ ]

December 2023

25 Monday
Christmas

☐
☐
☐
☐
☐
☐

26 Tuesday
Boxing Day
(CAN, UK, AUS, NZ)
Kwanzaa begins
O Full Moon

☐
☐
☐
☐
☐
☐

27 Wednesday

☐
☐
☐
☐
☐
☐

DECEMBER

S	M	T	W	T	F	S
					1	2
3	4	5	6	7	8	9
10	11	12	13	14	15	16
17	18	19	20	21	22	23
24	25	26	27	28	29	30
31						

28 Thursday

- [ ]
- [ ]
- [ ]
- [ ]
- [ ]
- [ ]

29 Friday

- [ ]
- [ ]
- [ ]
- [ ]
- [ ]
- [ ]

30 Saturday

- [ ]
- [ ]
- [ ]
- [ ]
- [ ]
- [ ]

31 Sunday

- [ ]
- [ ]
- [ ]
- [ ]
- [ ]
- [ ]

2024

JANUARY
S	M	T	W	T	F	S
	1	2	3	4	5	6
7	8	9	10	11	12	13
14	15	16	17	18	19	20
21	22	23	24	25	26	27
28	29	30	31			

FEBRUARY
S	M	T	W	T	F	S
				1	2	3
4	5	6	7	8	9	10
11	12	13	14	15	16	17
18	19	20	21	22	23	24
25	26	27	28	29		

MARCH
S	M	T	W	T	F	S
					1	2
3	4	5	6	7	8	9
10	11	12	13	14	15	16
17	18	19	20	21	22	23
24	25	26	27	28	29	30
31						

APRIL
S	M	T	W	T	F	S
	1	2	3	4	5	6
7	8	9	10	11	12	13
14	15	16	17	18	19	20
21	22	23	24	25	26	27
28	29	30				

MAY
S	M	T	W	T	F	S
			1	2	3	4
5	6	7	8	9	10	11
12	13	14	15	16	17	18
19	20	21	22	23	24	25
26	27	28	29	30	31	

JUNE
S	M	T	W	T	F	S
						1
2	3	4	5	6	7	8
9	10	11	12	13	14	15
16	17	18	19	20	21	22
23	24	25	26	27	28	29
30						

JULY
S	M	T	W	T	F	S
	1	2	3	4	5	6
7	8	9	10	11	12	13
14	15	16	17	18	19	20
21	22	23	24	25	26	27
28	29	30	31			

AUGUST
S	M	T	W	T	F	S
				1	2	3
4	5	6	7	8	9	10
11	12	13	14	15	16	17
18	19	20	21	22	23	24
25	26	27	28	29	30	31

SEPTEMBER
S	M	T	W	T	F	S
1	2	3	4	5	6	7
8	9	10	11	12	13	14
15	16	17	18	19	20	21
22	23	24	25	26	27	28
29	30					

OCTOBER
S	M	T	W	T	F	S
		1	2	3	4	5
6	7	8	9	10	11	12
13	14	15	16	17	18	19
20	21	22	23	24	25	26
27	28	29	30	31		

NOVEMBER
S	M	T	W	T	F	S
					1	2
3	4	5	6	7	8	9
10	11	12	13	14	15	16
17	18	19	20	21	22	23
24	25	26	27	28	29	30

DECEMBER
S	M	T	W	T	F	S
1	2	3	4	5	6	7
8	9	10	11	12	13	14
15	16	17	18	19	20	21
22	23	24	25	26	27	28
29	30	31				

Notes

_____
_____
_____
_____
_____
_____
_____
_____
_____
_____
_____
_____
_____
_____
_____
_____
_____
_____
_____
_____
_____
_____
_____
_____
_____
_____
_____
_____
_____

January

SUNDAY	MONDAY	TUESDAY	WEDNESDAY
31	1 New Year's Day	2	3
7	8	9	10
14	15 Martin Luther King Jr.'s Birthday	16	17
21	22	23	24
28	29	30	31

2024

THURSDAY	FRIDAY	SATURDAY	NOTES
4	5	6	
11	12	13	
● New Moon			
18	19	20	
25	26	27	
○ Full Moon	Australia Day		
1	2	3	

S	M	T	W	T	F	S
					1	2
3	4	5	6	7	8	9
10	11	12	13	14	15	16
17	18	19	20	21	22	23
24	25	26	27	28	29	30
31						

FEBRUARY

S	M	T	W	T	F	S
				1	2	3
4	5	6	7	8	9	10
11	12	13	14	15	16	17
18	19	20	21	22	23	24
25	26	27	28	29		

January 2024

1 Monday
New Year's Day 2024

☐
☐
☐
☐
☐
☐

2 Tuesday

☐
☐
☐
☐
☐
☐

3 Wednesday

☐
☐
☐
☐
☐
☐

JANUARY

S	M	T	W	T	F	S
	1	2	3	4	5	6
7	8	9	10	11	12	13
14	15	16	17	18	19	20
21	22	23	24	25	26	27
28	29	30	31			

4 Thursday

- [ ]
- [ ]
- [ ]
- [ ]
- [ ]
- [ ]

5 Friday

- [ ]
- [ ]
- [ ]
- [ ]
- [ ]
- [ ]

6 Saturday

- [ ]
- [ ]
- [ ]
- [ ]
- [ ]
- [ ]

7 Sunday

- [ ]
- [ ]
- [ ]
- [ ]
- [ ]
- [ ]

January 2024

8 Monday

- [ ]
- [ ]
- [ ]
- [ ]
- [ ]
- [ ]

9 Tuesday

- [ ]
- [ ]
- [ ]
- [ ]
- [ ]
- [ ]

10 Wednesday

- [ ]
- [ ]
- [ ]
- [ ]
- [ ]
- [ ]

JANUARY

S	M	T	W	T	F	S
	1	2	3	4	5	6
7	8	9	10	11	12	13
14	15	16	17	18	19	20
21	22	23	24	25	26	27
28	29	30	31			

11 Thursday
● New Moon

- [ ]
- [ ]
- [ ]
- [ ]
- [ ]
- [ ]

12 Friday

- [ ]
- [ ]
- [ ]
- [ ]
- [ ]
- [ ]

13 Saturday

- [ ]
- [ ]
- [ ]
- [ ]
- [ ]
- [ ]

14 Sunday

- [ ]
- [ ]
- [ ]
- [ ]
- [ ]
- [ ]

January 2024

15 Monday   Martin Luther King Jr.'s Birthday

- [ ]
- [ ]
- [ ]
- [ ]
- [ ]
- [ ]

16 Tuesday

- [ ]
- [ ]
- [ ]
- [ ]
- [ ]
- [ ]

17 Wednesday

- [ ]
- [ ]
- [ ]
- [ ]
- [ ]
- [ ]

JANUARY

S	M	T	W	T	F	S
	1	2	3	4	5	6
7	8	9	10	11	12	13
14	15	16	17	18	19	20
21	22	23	24	25	26	27
28	29	30	31			

18 Thursday

- [ ]
- [ ]
- [ ]
- [ ]
- [ ]
- [ ]

19 Friday

- [ ]
- [ ]
- [ ]
- [ ]
- [ ]
- [ ]

20 Saturday

- [ ]
- [ ]
- [ ]
- [ ]
- [ ]
- [ ]

21 Sunday

- [ ]
- [ ]
- [ ]
- [ ]
- [ ]
- [ ]

January 2024

22 Monday

23 Tuesday

24 Wednesday

JANUARY

S	M	T	W	T	F	S
	1	2	3	4	5	6
7	8	9	10	11	12	13
14	15	16	17	18	19	20
21	22	23	24	25	26	27
28	29	30	31			

25 Thursday

○ Full Moon

☐
☐
☐
☐
☐
☐

26 Friday

Australia Day

☐
☐
☐
☐
☐
☐

27 Saturday

☐
☐
☐
☐
☐
☐

28 Sunday

☐
☐
☐
☐
☐
☐

 February

SUNDAY	MONDAY	TUESDAY	WEDNESDAY
28	29	30	31
4	5	6 Waitangi Day (New Zealand)	7
11	12 Lincoln's Birthday	13	14 Valentine's Day Ash Wednesday
18	19 Presidents' Day	20	21
25	26	27	28

2024

THURSDAY	FRIDAY	SATURDAY	NOTES
1	2	3	
	Groundhog Day		
8	9	10	
	● New Moon	Chinese New Year	
15	16	17	
22	23	24	
Washington's Birthday		○ Full Moon	
29	1	2	

JANUARY

S	M	T	W	T	F	S
	1	2	3	4	5	6
7	8	9	10	11	12	13
14	15	16	17	18	19	20
21	22	23	24	25	26	27
28	29	30	31			

MARCH

S	M	T	W	T	F	S
					1	2
3	4	5	6	7	8	9
10	11	12	13	14	15	16
17	18	19	20	21	22	23
24	25	26	27	28	29	30
31						

January 2024

29 Monday

- [ ]
- [ ]
- [ ]
- [ ]
- [ ]
- [ ]

30 Tuesday

- [ ]
- [ ]
- [ ]
- [ ]
- [ ]
- [ ]

31 Wednesday

- [ ]
- [ ]
- [ ]
- [ ]
- [ ]
- [ ]

February

FEBRUARY

S	M	T	W	T	F	S
				1	2	3
4	5	6	7	8	9	10
11	12	13	14	15	16	17
18	19	20	21	22	23	24
25	26	27	28	29		

1 Thursday

- [ ]
- [ ]
- [ ]
- [ ]
- [ ]
- [ ]

2 Friday   Groundhog Day

- [ ]
- [ ]
- [ ]
- [ ]
- [ ]
- [ ]

3 Saturday

- [ ]
- [ ]
- [ ]
- [ ]
- [ ]
- [ ]

4 Sunday

- [ ]
- [ ]
- [ ]
- [ ]
- [ ]
- [ ]

February 2024

5 Monday

- [ ]
- [ ]
- [ ]
- [ ]
- [ ]
- [ ]

6 Tuesday   Waitangi Day (New Zealand)

- [ ]
- [ ]
- [ ]
- [ ]
- [ ]
- [ ]

7 Wednesday

- [ ]
- [ ]
- [ ]
- [ ]
- [ ]
- [ ]

FEBRUARY

S	M	T	W	T	F	S
				1	2	3
4	5	6	7	8	9	10
11	12	13	14	15	16	17
18	19	20	21	22	23	24
25	26	27	28	29		

8 Thursday

- [ ]
- [ ]
- [ ]
- [ ]
- [ ]
- [ ]

9 Friday

● New Moon

- [ ]
- [ ]
- [ ]
- [ ]
- [ ]
- [ ]

10 Saturday   Chinese New Year

- [ ]
- [ ]
- [ ]
- [ ]
- [ ]
- [ ]

11 Sunday

- [ ]
- [ ]
- [ ]
- [ ]
- [ ]
- [ ]

February 2024

12 Monday   Lincoln's Birthday

13 Tuesday

Valentine's Day
Ash Wednesday

14 Wednesday

FEBRUARY

S	M	T	W	T	F	S
				1	2	3
4	5	6	7	8	9	10
11	12	13	14	15	16	17
18	19	20	21	22	23	24
25	26	27	28	29		

15 Thursday

- [ ]
- [ ]
- [ ]
- [ ]
- [ ]
- [ ]

16 Friday

- [ ]
- [ ]
- [ ]
- [ ]
- [ ]
- [ ]

17 Saturday

- [ ]
- [ ]
- [ ]
- [ ]
- [ ]
- [ ]

18 Sunday

- [ ]
- [ ]
- [ ]
- [ ]
- [ ]
- [ ]

February 2024

19 Monday Presidents' Day

- [ ]
- [ ]
- [ ]
- [ ]
- [ ]
- [ ]

20 Tuesday

- [ ]
- [ ]
- [ ]
- [ ]
- [ ]
- [ ]

21 Wednesday

- [ ]
- [ ]
- [ ]
- [ ]
- [ ]
- [ ]

FEBRUARY

S	M	T	W	T	F	S
				1	2	3
4	5	6	7	8	9	10
11	12	13	14	15	16	17
18	19	20	21	22	23	24
25	26	27	28	29		

22 Thursday

Washington's Birthday

- [ ]
- [ ]
- [ ]
- [ ]
- [ ]
- [ ]

23 Friday

- [ ]
- [ ]
- [ ]
- [ ]
- [ ]
- [ ]

24 Saturday

○ Full Moon

- [ ]
- [ ]
- [ ]
- [ ]
- [ ]
- [ ]

25 Sunday

- [ ]
- [ ]
- [ ]
- [ ]
- [ ]
- [ ]

February 2024

26 Monday

- [ ]
- [ ]
- [ ]
- [ ]
- [ ]
- [ ]

27 Tuesday

- [ ]
- [ ]
- [ ]
- [ ]
- [ ]
- [ ]

28 Wednesday

- [ ]
- [ ]
- [ ]
- [ ]
- [ ]
- [ ]

March

MARCH

S	M	T	W	T	F	S
					1	2
3	4	5	6	7	8	9
10	11	12	13	14	15	16
17	18	19	20	21	22	23
24	25	26	27	28	29	30
31						

29 Thursday

- [ ]
- [ ]
- [ ]
- [ ]
- [ ]
- [ ]

1 Friday

- [ ]
- [ ]
- [ ]
- [ ]
- [ ]
- [ ]

2 Saturday

- [ ]
- [ ]
- [ ]
- [ ]
- [ ]
- [ ]

3 Sunday

- [ ]
- [ ]
- [ ]
- [ ]
- [ ]
- [ ]

 March

SUNDAY	MONDAY	TUESDAY	WEDNESDAY
25	26	27	28
3	4 Labour Day (W. Australia)	5	6
10 Daylight Saving begins Mother's Day (UK) ● New Moon	11 Commonwealth Day (CAN, UK, AUS) Canberra Day (ACT) Labour Day (Victoria)	12	13
17 St. Patrick's Day	18	19 Vernal Equinox	20
24/31 Palm Sunday (24th) Easter Sunday (31st)	25 ○ Full Moon	26	27

2024

THURSDAY	FRIDAY	SATURDAY	NOTES
29	1	2	
7	8 International Women's Day	9	
14	15	16	
21	22	23	
28	29 Good Friday	30	

FEBRUARY

S	M	T	W	T	F	S
				1	2	3
4	5	6	7	8	9	10
11	12	13	14	15	16	17
18	19	20	21	22	23	24
25	26	27	28	29		

APRIL

S	M	T	W	T	F	S
	1	2	3	4	5	6
7	8	9	10	11	12	13
14	15	16	17	18	19	20
21	22	23	24	25	26	27
28	29	30				

March 2024

4 Monday   Labour Day (W. Australia)

☐
☐
☐
☐
☐
☐

5 Tuesday

☐
☐
☐
☐
☐
☐

6 Wednesday

☐
☐
☐
☐
☐
☐

MARCH

S	M	T	W	T	F	S
					1	2
3	4	5	6	7	8	9
10	11	12	13	14	15	16
17	18	19	20	21	22	23
24	25	26	27	28	29	30
31						

7 Thursday

- [ ]
- [ ]
- [ ]
- [ ]
- [ ]
- [ ]

8 Friday

International Women's Day

- [ ]
- [ ]
- [ ]
- [ ]
- [ ]
- [ ]

Daylight Saving begins

Mother's Day (UK)

9 Saturday

- [ ]
- [ ]
- [ ]
- [ ]
- [ ]
- [ ]

10 Sunday

● New Moon

- [ ]
- [ ]
- [ ]
- [ ]
- [ ]
- [ ]

March 2024

11 Monday

12 Tuesday

13 Wednesday

MARCH

S	M	T	W	T	F	S
					1	2
3	4	5	6	7	8	9
10	11	12	13	14	15	16
17	18	19	20	21	22	23
24	25	26	27	28	29	30
31						

14 Thursday

- [ ]
- [ ]
- [ ]
- [ ]
- [ ]
- [ ]

15 Friday

- [ ]
- [ ]
- [ ]
- [ ]
- [ ]
- [ ]

16 Saturday

- [ ]
- [ ]
- [ ]
- [ ]
- [ ]
- [ ]

17 Sunday   St. Patrick's Day

- [ ]
- [ ]
- [ ]
- [ ]
- [ ]
- [ ]

March 2024

18 Monday

- [ ]
- [ ]
- [ ]
- [ ]
- [ ]
- [ ]

19 Tuesday   Vernal Equinox

- [ ]
- [ ]
- [ ]
- [ ]
- [ ]
- [ ]

20 Wednesday

- [ ]
- [ ]
- [ ]
- [ ]
- [ ]
- [ ]

MARCH

S	M	T	W	T	F	S
					1	2
3	4	5	6	7	8	9
10	11	12	13	14	15	16
17	18	19	20	21	22	23
24	25	26	27	28	29	30
31						

21 Thursday

- [ ]
- [ ]
- [ ]
- [ ]
- [ ]
- [ ]

22 Friday

- [ ]
- [ ]
- [ ]
- [ ]
- [ ]
- [ ]

23 Saturday

- [ ]
- [ ]
- [ ]
- [ ]
- [ ]
- [ ]

24 Sunday   Palm Sunday

- [ ]
- [ ]
- [ ]
- [ ]
- [ ]
- [ ]

March 2024

25 Monday   O Full Moon

26 Tuesday

27 Wednesday

MARCH

S	M	T	W	T	F	S
					1	2
3	4	5	6	7	8	9
10	11	12	13	14	15	16
17	18	19	20	21	22	23
24	25	26	27	28	29	30
31						

28 Thursday

☐
☐
☐
☐
☐
☐

29 Friday   Good Friday

☐
☐
☐
☐
☐
☐

30 Saturday

☐
☐
☐
☐
☐
☐

31 Sunday   Easter Sunday

☐
☐
☐
☐
☐
☐

 April

SUNDAY	MONDAY	TUESDAY	WEDNESDAY
31	1 Easter Monday (CAN, UK, AUS, NZ)	2	3
7	8 ● New Moon	9	10
14	15	16	17
21	22 Passover begins at sundown Earth Day	23 ○ Full Moon	24
28	29	30	1

❋➤ 2024 ❀❀

THURSDAY	FRIDAY	SATURDAY	NOTES
4	5	6	
11	12	13	
18	19	20	
25 ANZAC Day (Australia, NZ)	26 Arbor Day	27	
2	3	4	

MARCH

S	M	T	W	T	F	S
					1	2
3	4	5	6	7	8	9
10	11	12	13	14	15	16
17	18	19	20	21	22	23
24	25	26	27	28	29	30
31						

MAY

S	M	T	W	T	F	S
			1	2	3	4
5	6	7	8	9	10	11
12	13	14	15	16	17	18
19	20	21	22	23	24	25
26	27	28	29	30	31	

April 2024

1 Monday
Easter Monday (CAN, UK, AUS, NZ)

- [ ]
- [ ]
- [ ]
- [ ]
- [ ]
- [ ]

2 Tuesday

- [ ]
- [ ]
- [ ]
- [ ]
- [ ]
- [ ]

3 Wednesday

- [ ]
- [ ]
- [ ]
- [ ]
- [ ]
- [ ]

APRIL

S	M	T	W	T	F	S
	1	2	3	4	5	6
7	8	9	10	11	12	13
14	15	16	17	18	19	20
21	22	23	24	25	26	27
28	29	30				

4 Thursday

☐
☐
☐
☐
☐
☐

5 Friday

☐
☐
☐
☐
☐
☐

6 Saturday

☐
☐
☐
☐
☐
☐

7 Sunday

☐
☐
☐
☐
☐
☐

April 2024

8 Monday
● New Moon

- [ ]
- [ ]
- [ ]
- [ ]
- [ ]
- [ ]

9 Tuesday

- [ ]
- [ ]
- [ ]
- [ ]
- [ ]
- [ ]

10 Wednesday

- [ ]
- [ ]
- [ ]
- [ ]
- [ ]
- [ ]

APRIL

S	M	T	W	T	F	S
	1	2	3	4	5	6
7	8	9	10	11	12	13
14	15	16	17	18	19	20
21	22	23	24	25	26	27
28	29	30				

11 Thursday

- [ ]
- [ ]
- [ ]
- [ ]
- [ ]
- [ ]

12 Friday

- [ ]
- [ ]
- [ ]
- [ ]
- [ ]
- [ ]

13 Saturday

- [ ]
- [ ]
- [ ]
- [ ]
- [ ]
- [ ]

14 Sunday

- [ ]
- [ ]
- [ ]
- [ ]
- [ ]
- [ ]

April 2024

15 Monday

16 Tuesday

17 Wednesday

APRIL

S	M	T	W	T	F	S
	1	2	3	4	5	6
7	8	9	10	11	12	13
14	15	16	17	18	19	20
21	22	23	24	25	26	27
28	29	30				

18 Thursday

- [ ]
- [ ]
- [ ]
- [ ]
- [ ]
- [ ]

19 Friday

- [ ]
- [ ]
- [ ]
- [ ]
- [ ]
- [ ]

20 Saturday

- [ ]
- [ ]
- [ ]
- [ ]
- [ ]
- [ ]

21 Sunday

- [ ]
- [ ]
- [ ]
- [ ]
- [ ]
- [ ]

April 2024

22 Monday

Passover begins at sundown

Earth Day

- [ ]
- [ ]
- [ ]
- [ ]
- [ ]
- [ ]

23 Tuesday

O Full Moon

- [ ]
- [ ]
- [ ]
- [ ]
- [ ]
- [ ]

24 Wednesday

- [ ]
- [ ]
- [ ]
- [ ]
- [ ]
- [ ]

APRIL

S	M	T	W	T	F	S
	1	2	3	4	5	6
7	8	9	10	11	12	13
14	15	16	17	18	19	20
21	22	23	24	25	26	27
28	29	30				

25 Thursday

ANZAC Day (Australia, NZ)

☐ _____
☐ _____
☐ _____
☐ _____
☐ _____
☐ _____

26 Friday

Arbor Day

☐ _____
☐ _____
☐ _____
☐ _____
☐ _____
☐ _____

27 Saturday

☐ _____
☐ _____
☐ _____
☐ _____
☐ _____
☐ _____

28 Sunday

☐ _____
☐ _____
☐ _____
☐ _____
☐ _____
☐ _____

May

SUNDAY	MONDAY	TUESDAY	WEDNESDAY
28	29	30	1 May Day
5 Holocaust Remembrance Day begins at sundown	6 Bank Holiday (UK) Labour Day (Queensland)	7 ● New Moon	8
12 Mother's Day (US, CAN, AUS, NZ)	13	14	15
19	20 Victoria Day (Canada)	21	22
26	27 Memorial Day Bank Holiday (UK)	28	29

2024

THURSDAY	FRIDAY	SATURDAY	NOTES
2	3	4	
9	10	11	
16	17	18 Armed Forces Day	
23 O Full Moon	24	25	
30	31	1	

APRIL

S	M	T	W	T	F	S
	1	2	3	4	5	6
7	8	9	10	11	12	13
14	15	16	17	18	19	20
21	22	23	24	25	26	27
28	29	30				

JUNE

S	M	T	W	T	F	S
						1
2	3	4	5	6	7	8
9	10	11	12	13	14	15
16	17	18	19	20	21	22
23	24	25	26	27	28	29
30						

April 2024

29 Monday

- [ ]
- [ ]
- [ ]
- [ ]
- [ ]
- [ ]

30 Tuesday

- [ ]
- [ ]
- [ ]
- [ ]
- [ ]
- [ ]

1 Wednesday   May Day

- [ ]
- [ ]
- [ ]
- [ ]
- [ ]
- [ ]

May

MAY

S	M	T	W	T	F	S
			1	2	3	4
5	6	7	8	9	10	11
12	13	14	15	16	17	18
19	20	21	22	23	24	25
26	27	28	29	30	31	

2 Thursday

☐
☐
☐
☐
☐
☐

3 Friday

☐
☐
☐
☐
☐
☐

4 Saturday

☐
☐
☐
☐
☐
☐

5 Sunday

Holocaust
Remembrance Day
begins at sundown

☐
☐
☐
☐
☐
☐

May 2024

6 Monday

Bank Holiday (UK)
Labour Day (Queensland)

- [ ]
- [ ]
- [ ]
- [ ]
- [ ]
- [ ]

7 Tuesday

● New Moon

- [ ]
- [ ]
- [ ]
- [ ]
- [ ]
- [ ]

8 Wednesday

- [ ]
- [ ]
- [ ]
- [ ]
- [ ]
- [ ]

MAY
S M T W T F S
             1 2 3 4
5 6 7 8 9 10 11
12 13 14 15 16 17 18
19 20 21 22 23 24 25
26 27 28 29 30 31

9 Thursday

- [ ]
- [ ]
- [ ]
- [ ]
- [ ]
- [ ]

10 Friday

- [ ]
- [ ]
- [ ]
- [ ]
- [ ]
- [ ]

11 Saturday

- [ ]
- [ ]
- [ ]
- [ ]
- [ ]
- [ ]

12 Sunday

Mother's Day
(US, CAN, AUS, NZ)

- [ ]
- [ ]
- [ ]
- [ ]
- [ ]
- [ ]

May 2024

13 Monday

14 Tuesday

15 Wednesday

MAY

S	M	T	W	T	F	S
			1	2	3	4
5	6	7	8	9	10	11
12	13	14	15	16	17	18
19	20	21	22	23	24	25
26	27	28	29	30	31	

16 Thursday

17 Friday

18 Saturday   Armed Forces Day

19 Sunday

May 2024

20 Monday   Victoria Day (Canada)

- [ ]
- [ ]
- [ ]
- [ ]
- [ ]
- [ ]

21 Tuesday

- [ ]
- [ ]
- [ ]
- [ ]
- [ ]
- [ ]

22 Wednesday

- [ ]
- [ ]
- [ ]
- [ ]
- [ ]
- [ ]

MAY

S	M	T	W	T	F	S
			1	2	3	4
5	6	7	8	9	10	11
12	13	14	15	16	17	18
19	20	21	22	23	24	25
26	27	28	29	30	31	

23 Thursday

○ Full Moon

- [ ]
- [ ]
- [ ]
- [ ]
- [ ]
- [ ]

24 Friday

- [ ]
- [ ]
- [ ]
- [ ]
- [ ]
- [ ]

25 Saturday

- [ ]
- [ ]
- [ ]
- [ ]
- [ ]
- [ ]

26 Sunday

- [ ]
- [ ]
- [ ]
- [ ]
- [ ]
- [ ]

May 2024

27 Monday

Memorial Day
Bank Holiday (UK)

☐
☐
☐
☐
☐
☐

28 Tuesday

☐
☐
☐
☐
☐
☐

29 Wednesday

☐
☐
☐
☐
☐
☐

June

S	M	T	W	T	F	S
						1
2	3	4	5	6	7	8
9	10	11	12	13	14	15
16	17	18	19	20	21	22
23	24	25	26	27	28	29
30						

30 Thursday

- [ ]
- [ ]
- [ ]
- [ ]
- [ ]
- [ ]

31 Friday

- [ ]
- [ ]
- [ ]
- [ ]
- [ ]
- [ ]

1 Saturday

- [ ]
- [ ]
- [ ]
- [ ]
- [ ]
- [ ]

2 Sunday

- [ ]
- [ ]
- [ ]
- [ ]
- [ ]
- [ ]

June

SUNDAY	MONDAY	TUESDAY	WEDNESDAY
26	27	28	29
2	3 King's Birthday (New Zealand)	4	5
9	10 King's Birthday (Australia)	11	12
16 Father's Day (US, Canada, UK)	17	18	19 Juneteenth
23/30	24	25	26

 2024

THURSDAY	FRIDAY	SATURDAY	NOTES
30	31	1	
6	7	8	
● New Moon			
13	14	15	
	Flag Day		
20	21	22	
Summer Solstice	○ Full Moon		
27	28	29	

MAY

S	M	T	W	T	F	S
			1	2	3	4
5	6	7	8	9	10	11
12	13	14	15	16	17	18
19	20	21	22	23	24	25
26	27	28	29	30	31	

JULY

S	M	T	W	T	F	S
	1	2	3	4	5	6
7	8	9	10	11	12	13
14	15	16	17	18	19	20
21	22	23	24	25	26	27
28	29	30	31			

June 2024

3 Monday

King's Birthday (New Zealand)

☐
☐
☐
☐
☐
☐

4 Tuesday

☐
☐
☐
☐
☐
☐

5 Wednesday

☐
☐
☐
☐
☐
☐

JUNE

S	M	T	W	T	F	S
						1
2	3	4	5	6	7	8
9	10	11	12	13	14	15
16	17	18	19	20	21	22
23	24	25	26	27	28	29
30						

6 Thursday

● New Moon

☐
☐
☐
☐
☐
☐

7 Friday

☐
☐
☐
☐
☐
☐

8 Saturday

☐
☐
☐
☐
☐
☐

9 Sunday

☐
☐
☐
☐
☐
☐

June 2024

10 Monday
King's Birthday (Australia)

☐
☐
☐
☐
☐
☐

11 Tuesday

☐
☐
☐
☐
☐
☐

12 Wednesday

☐
☐
☐
☐
☐
☐

JUNE

S	M	T	W	T	F	S
						1
2	3	4	5	6	7	8
9	10	11	12	13	14	15
16	17	18	19	20	21	22
23	24	25	26	27	28	29
30						

13 Thursday

14 Friday   Flag Day

15 Saturday

16 Sunday   Father's Day
(US, Canada, UK)

June 2024

17 Monday

☐
☐
☐
☐
☐
☐

18 Tuesday

☐
☐
☐
☐
☐
☐

19 Wednesday   Juneteenth

☐
☐
☐
☐
☐
☐

JUNE
S	M	T	W	T	F	S
						1
2	3	4	5	6	7	8
9	10	11	12	13	14	15
16	17	18	19	20	21	22
23	24	25	26	27	28	29
30						

20 Thursday

Summer Solstice

21 Friday

O Full Moon

22 Saturday

23 Sunday

June 2024

24 Monday

- [ ]
- [ ]
- [ ]
- [ ]
- [ ]
- [ ]

25 Tuesday

- [ ]
- [ ]
- [ ]
- [ ]
- [ ]
- [ ]

26 Wednesday

- [ ]
- [ ]
- [ ]
- [ ]
- [ ]
- [ ]

JUNE

S	M	T	W	T	F	S
						1
2	3	4	5	6	7	8
9	10	11	12	13	14	15
16	17	18	19	20	21	22
23	24	25	26	27	28	29
30						

27 Thursday

- [ ]
- [ ]
- [ ]
- [ ]
- [ ]
- [ ]

28 Friday

- [ ]
- [ ]
- [ ]
- [ ]
- [ ]
- [ ]

29 Saturday

- [ ]
- [ ]
- [ ]
- [ ]
- [ ]
- [ ]

30 Sunday

- [ ]
- [ ]
- [ ]
- [ ]
- [ ]
- [ ]

July

SUNDAY	MONDAY	TUESDAY	WEDNESDAY
30	1 Canada Day	2	3
7	8	9	10
14	15	16	17
21 ○ Full Moon	22	23	24
28	29	30	31

2024

THURSDAY	FRIDAY	SATURDAY	NOTES
4	5	6	_____
			_____
			_____
			_____
Independence Day	● New Moon		_____
11	12	13	_____
			_____
			_____
			_____
			_____
18	19	20	_____
			_____
			_____
			_____
25	26	27	_____
			_____

JUNE

S	M	T	W	T	F	S
						1
2	3	4	5	6	7	8
9	10	11	12	13	14	15
16	17	18	19	20	21	22
23	24	25	26	27	28	29
30						

| 1 | 2 | 3 |

AUGUST

S	M	T	W	T	F	S
				1	2	3
4	5	6	7	8	9	10
11	12	13	14	15	16	17
18	19	20	21	22	23	24
25	26	27	28	29	30	31

July 2024

1 Monday   Canada Day

☐
☐
☐
☐
☐
☐

2 Tuesday

☐
☐
☐
☐
☐
☐

3 Wednesday

☐
☐
☐
☐
☐
☐

JULY

S	M	T	W	T	F	S
	1	2	3	4	5	6
7	8	9	10	11	12	13
14	15	16	17	18	19	20
21	22	23	24	25	26	27
28	29	30	31			

4 Thursday

Independence Day

- [ ]
- [ ]
- [ ]
- [ ]
- [ ]
- [ ]

5 Friday

● New Moon

- [ ]
- [ ]
- [ ]
- [ ]
- [ ]
- [ ]

6 Saturday

- [ ]
- [ ]
- [ ]
- [ ]
- [ ]
- [ ]

7 Sunday

- [ ]
- [ ]
- [ ]
- [ ]
- [ ]
- [ ]

July 2024

8 Monday

- [ ]
- [ ]
- [ ]
- [ ]
- [ ]
- [ ]

9 Tuesday

- [ ]
- [ ]
- [ ]
- [ ]
- [ ]
- [ ]

10 Wednesday

- [ ]
- [ ]
- [ ]
- [ ]
- [ ]
- [ ]

JULY

S	M	T	W	T	F	S
	1	2	3	4	5	6
7	8	9	10	11	12	13
14	15	16	17	18	19	20
21	22	23	24	25	26	27
28	29	30	31			

11 Thursday

- [ ]
- [ ]
- [ ]
- [ ]
- [ ]
- [ ]

12 Friday

- [ ]
- [ ]
- [ ]
- [ ]
- [ ]
- [ ]

13 Saturday

- [ ]
- [ ]
- [ ]
- [ ]
- [ ]
- [ ]

14 Sunday

- [ ]
- [ ]
- [ ]
- [ ]
- [ ]
- [ ]

July 2024

15 Monday

- [ ]
- [ ]
- [ ]
- [ ]
- [ ]
- [ ]

16 Tuesday

- [ ]
- [ ]
- [ ]
- [ ]
- [ ]
- [ ]

17 Wednesday

- [ ]
- [ ]
- [ ]
- [ ]
- [ ]
- [ ]

JULY

S	M	T	W	T	F	S
	1	2	3	4	5	6
7	8	9	10	11	12	13
14	15	16	17	18	19	20
21	22	23	24	25	26	27
28	29	30	31			

18 Thursday

- [ ]
- [ ]
- [ ]
- [ ]
- [ ]
- [ ]

19 Friday

- [ ]
- [ ]
- [ ]
- [ ]
- [ ]
- [ ]

20 Saturday

- [ ]
- [ ]
- [ ]
- [ ]
- [ ]
- [ ]

21 Sunday   ○ Full Moon

- [ ]
- [ ]
- [ ]
- [ ]
- [ ]
- [ ]

July 2024

22 Monday

☐
☐
☐
☐
☐
☐

23 Tuesday

☐
☐
☐
☐
☐
☐

24 Wednesday

☐
☐
☐
☐
☐
☐

JULY

S	M	T	W	T	F	S
	1	2	3	4	5	6
7	8	9	10	11	12	13
14	15	16	17	18	19	20
21	22	23	24	25	26	27
28	29	30	31			

25 Thursday

- [ ]
- [ ]
- [ ]
- [ ]
- [ ]
- [ ]

26 Friday

- [ ]
- [ ]
- [ ]
- [ ]
- [ ]
- [ ]

27 Saturday

- [ ]
- [ ]
- [ ]
- [ ]
- [ ]
- [ ]

28 Sunday

- [ ]
- [ ]
- [ ]
- [ ]
- [ ]
- [ ]

 August

SUNDAY	MONDAY	TUESDAY	WEDNESDAY
28	29	30	31
4 ● New Moon	5 Bank Holiday (NSW) Civic Holiday (Canada)	6	7
11	12	13	14
18	19 ○ Full Moon	20	21
25	26 Bank Holiday (UK)	27	28

 # 2024

THURSDAY	FRIDAY	SATURDAY	NOTES
1	2	3	
8	9	10	
15	16	17	
22	23	24	
29	30	31	

JULY

S	M	T	W	T	F	S
	1	2	3	4	5	6
7	8	9	10	11	12	13
14	15	16	17	18	19	20
21	22	23	24	25	26	27
28	29	30	31			

SEPTEMBER

S	M	T	W	T	F	S
1	2	3	4	5	6	7
8	9	10	11	12	13	14
15	16	17	18	19	20	21
22	23	24	25	26	27	28
29	30					

July 2024

29 Monday

- [ ]
- [ ]
- [ ]
- [ ]
- [ ]
- [ ]

30 Tuesday

- [ ]
- [ ]
- [ ]
- [ ]
- [ ]
- [ ]

31 Wednesday

- [ ]
- [ ]
- [ ]
- [ ]
- [ ]
- [ ]

August

AUGUST

S	M	T	W	T	F	S
				1	2	3
4	5	6	7	8	9	10
11	12	13	14	15	16	17
18	19	20	21	22	23	24
25	26	27	28	29	30	31

1 Thursday

- [ ]
- [ ]
- [ ]
- [ ]
- [ ]
- [ ]

2 Friday

- [ ]
- [ ]
- [ ]
- [ ]
- [ ]
- [ ]

3 Saturday

- [ ]
- [ ]
- [ ]
- [ ]
- [ ]
- [ ]

4 Sunday ● New Moon

- [ ]
- [ ]
- [ ]
- [ ]
- [ ]
- [ ]

August 2024

5 Monday

- [ ]
- [ ]
- [ ]
- [ ]
- [ ]
- [ ]

6 Tuesday

- [ ]
- [ ]
- [ ]
- [ ]
- [ ]
- [ ]

7 Wednesday

- [ ]
- [ ]
- [ ]
- [ ]
- [ ]
- [ ]

AUGUST

S	M	T	W	T	F	S
				1	2	3
4	5	6	7	8	9	10
11	12	13	14	15	16	17
18	19	20	21	22	23	24
25	26	27	28	29	30	31

8 Thursday

☐
☐
☐
☐
☐
☐

9 Friday

☐
☐
☐
☐
☐
☐

10 Saturday

☐
☐
☐
☐
☐
☐

11 Sunday

☐
☐
☐
☐
☐
☐

August 2024

12 Monday

- [ ]
- [ ]
- [ ]
- [ ]
- [ ]
- [ ]

13 Tuesday

- [ ]
- [ ]
- [ ]
- [ ]
- [ ]
- [ ]

14 Wednesday

- [ ]
- [ ]
- [ ]
- [ ]
- [ ]
- [ ]

AUGUST

S	M	T	W	T	F	S
				1	2	3
4	5	6	7	8	9	10
11	12	13	14	15	16	17
18	19	20	21	22	23	24
25	26	27	28	29	30	31

15 Thursday

- [ ]
- [ ]
- [ ]
- [ ]
- [ ]
- [ ]

16 Friday

- [ ]
- [ ]
- [ ]
- [ ]
- [ ]
- [ ]

17 Saturday

- [ ]
- [ ]
- [ ]
- [ ]
- [ ]
- [ ]

18 Sunday

- [ ]
- [ ]
- [ ]
- [ ]
- [ ]
- [ ]

August 2024

19 Monday   O Full Moon

☐
☐
☐
☐
☐
☐

20 Tuesday

☐
☐
☐
☐
☐
☐

21 Wednesday

☐
☐
☐
☐
☐
☐

AUGUST

S	M	T	W	T	F	S
				1	2	3
4	5	6	7	8	9	10
11	12	13	14	15	16	17
18	19	20	21	22	23	24
25	26	27	28	29	30	31

22 Thursday

23 Friday

24 Saturday

25 Sunday

August 2024

26 Monday   Bank Holiday (UK)

- [ ]
- [ ]
- [ ]
- [ ]
- [ ]
- [ ]

27 Tuesday

- [ ]
- [ ]
- [ ]
- [ ]
- [ ]
- [ ]

28 Wednesday

- [ ]
- [ ]
- [ ]
- [ ]
- [ ]
- [ ]

September

SEPTEMBER

S	M	T	W	T	F	S
1	2	3	4	5	6	7
8	9	10	11	12	13	14
15	16	17	18	19	20	21
22	23	24	25	26	27	28
29	30					

29 Thursday

☐
☐
☐
☐
☐
☐

30 Friday

☐
☐
☐
☐
☐
☐

31 Saturday

☐
☐
☐
☐
☐
☐

1 Sunday

Father's Day
(Australia, NZ)

☐
☐
☐
☐
☐
☐

September

SUNDAY	MONDAY	TUESDAY	WEDNESDAY
1 Father's Day (Australia, NZ)	2 Labor Day (US, Canada) ● New Moon	3	4
8	9	10	11 Patriot Day
15	16	17 ○ Full Moon	18
22 Autumnal Equinox	23 King's Birthday (W. Australia)	24	25
29	30	1	2

 2024

THURSDAY	FRIDAY	SATURDAY	NOTES
5	6	7	
12	13	14	
19	20	21 UN International Day of Peace	
26	27	28	
3	4	5	

AUGUST

S	M	T	W	T	F	S
				1	2	3
4	5	6	7	8	9	10
11	12	13	14	15	16	17
18	19	20	21	22	23	24
25	26	27	28	29	30	31

OCTOBER

S	M	T	W	T	F	S
		1	2	3	4	5
6	7	8	9	10	11	12
13	14	15	16	17	18	19
20	21	22	23	24	25	26
27	28	29	30	31		

September 2024

2 Monday ● New Moon

- [ ]
- [ ]
- [ ]
- [ ]
- [ ]
- [ ]

3 Tuesday

- [ ]
- [ ]
- [ ]
- [ ]
- [ ]
- [ ]

4 Wednesday

- [ ]
- [ ]
- [ ]
- [ ]
- [ ]
- [ ]

SEPTEMBER

S	M	T	W	T	F	S
1	2	3	4	5	6	7
8	9	10	11	12	13	14
15	16	17	18	19	20	21
22	23	24	25	26	27	28
29	30					

5 Thursday

- [ ]
- [ ]
- [ ]
- [ ]
- [ ]
- [ ]

6 Friday

- [ ]
- [ ]
- [ ]
- [ ]
- [ ]
- [ ]

7 Saturday

- [ ]
- [ ]
- [ ]
- [ ]
- [ ]
- [ ]

8 Sunday

- [ ]
- [ ]
- [ ]
- [ ]
- [ ]
- [ ]

September 2024

9 Monday

☐
☐
☐
☐
☐
☐

10 Tuesday

☐
☐
☐
☐
☐
☐

11 Wednesday   Patriot Day

☐
☐
☐
☐
☐
☐

SEPTEMBER

S	M	T	W	T	F	S
1	2	3	4	5	6	7
8	9	10	11	12	13	14
15	16	17	18	19	20	21
22	23	24	25	26	27	28
29	30					

12 Thursday

- [ ]
- [ ]
- [ ]
- [ ]
- [ ]
- [ ]

13 Friday

- [ ]
- [ ]
- [ ]
- [ ]
- [ ]
- [ ]

14 Saturday

- [ ]
- [ ]
- [ ]
- [ ]
- [ ]
- [ ]

15 Sunday

- [ ]
- [ ]
- [ ]
- [ ]
- [ ]
- [ ]

September 2024

16 Monday

- [ ]
- [ ]
- [ ]
- [ ]
- [ ]
- [ ]

17 Tuesday

O Full Moon

- [ ]
- [ ]
- [ ]
- [ ]
- [ ]
- [ ]

18 Wednesday

- [ ]
- [ ]
- [ ]
- [ ]
- [ ]
- [ ]

SEPTEMBER

S	M	T	W	T	F	S
1	2	3	4	5	6	7
8	9	10	11	12	13	14
15	16	17	18	19	20	21
22	23	24	25	26	27	28
29	30					

19 Thursday

- [ ]
- [ ]
- [ ]
- [ ]
- [ ]
- [ ]

20 Friday

- [ ]
- [ ]
- [ ]
- [ ]
- [ ]
- [ ]

21 Saturday

UN International
Day of Peace

- [ ]
- [ ]
- [ ]
- [ ]
- [ ]
- [ ]

22 Sunday

Autumnal Equinox

- [ ]
- [ ]
- [ ]
- [ ]
- [ ]
- [ ]

September 2024

23 Monday
King's Birthday (W. Australia)

- [ ]
- [ ]
- [ ]
- [ ]
- [ ]
- [ ]

24 Tuesday

- [ ]
- [ ]
- [ ]
- [ ]
- [ ]
- [ ]

25 Wednesday

- [ ]
- [ ]
- [ ]
- [ ]
- [ ]
- [ ]

SEPTEMBER

S	M	T	W	T	F	S
	1	2	3	4	5	6	7
8	9	10	11	12	13	14
15	16	17	18	19	20	21
22	23	24	25	26	27	28
29	30					

26 Thursday

- ☐
- ☐
- ☐
- ☐
- ☐
- ☐

27 Friday

- ☐
- ☐
- ☐
- ☐
- ☐
- ☐

28 Saturday

- ☐
- ☐
- ☐
- ☐
- ☐
- ☐

29 Sunday

- ☐
- ☐
- ☐
- ☐
- ☐
- ☐

October

SUNDAY	MONDAY	TUESDAY	WEDNESDAY
29	30	1	2 Rosh Hashanah begins at sundown ● New Moon
6	7 Labour Day (ACT, NSW, SA) King's Birthday (Queensland)	8	9
13	14 Indigenous Peoples' Day (observed) Columbus Day (observed) Thanksgiving (Canada)	15	16
20	21	22	23
27	28 Labour Day (New Zealand)	29	30

2024

THURSDAY	FRIDAY	SATURDAY	NOTES
3	4	5	
10	11	12	
	Yom Kippur begins at sundown		
17	18	19	
○ Full Moon			
24	25	26	
31	1	2	
Halloween			

SEPTEMBER

S	M	T	W	T	F	S
1	2	3	4	5	6	7
8	9	10	11	12	13	14
15	16	17	18	19	20	21
22	23	24	25	26	27	28
29	30					

NOVEMBER

S	M	T	W	T	F	S
					1	2
3	4	5	6	7	8	9
10	11	12	13	14	15	16
17	18	19	20	21	22	23
24	25	26	27	28	29	30

September 2024

30 Monday

- [ ]
- [ ]
- [ ]
- [ ]
- [ ]
- [ ]

1 Tuesday

- [ ]
- [ ]
- [ ]
- [ ]
- [ ]
- [ ]

Rosh Hashanah begins at sundown

● New Moon

2 Wednesday

- [ ]
- [ ]
- [ ]
- [ ]
- [ ]
- [ ]

October

OCTOBER

S	M	T	W	T	F	S
		1	2	3	4	5
6	7	8	9	10	11	12
13	14	15	16	17	18	19
20	21	22	23	24	25	26
27	28	29	30	31		

3 Thursday

- [ ]
- [ ]
- [ ]
- [ ]
- [ ]
- [ ]

4 Friday

- [ ]
- [ ]
- [ ]
- [ ]
- [ ]
- [ ]

5 Saturday

- [ ]
- [ ]
- [ ]
- [ ]
- [ ]
- [ ]

6 Sunday

- [ ]
- [ ]
- [ ]
- [ ]
- [ ]
- [ ]

October 2024

7 Monday

Labour Day (ACT, NSW, SA)
King's Birthday (Queensland)

- [ ]
- [ ]
- [ ]
- [ ]
- [ ]
- [ ]

8 Tuesday

- [ ]
- [ ]
- [ ]
- [ ]
- [ ]
- [ ]

9 Wednesday

- [ ]
- [ ]
- [ ]
- [ ]
- [ ]
- [ ]

OCTOBER

S	M	T	W	T	F	S
		1	2	3	4	5
6	7	8	9	10	11	12
13	14	15	16	17	18	19
20	21	22	23	24	25	26
27	28	29	30	31		

10 Thursday

- [ ]
- [ ]
- [ ]
- [ ]
- [ ]
- [ ]

11 Friday

Yom Kippur
begins at sundown

- [ ]
- [ ]
- [ ]
- [ ]
- [ ]
- [ ]

12 Saturday

- [ ]
- [ ]
- [ ]
- [ ]
- [ ]
- [ ]

13 Sunday

- [ ]
- [ ]
- [ ]
- [ ]
- [ ]
- [ ]

October 2024

14 Monday

☐
☐
☐
☐
☐
☐

15 Tuesday

☐
☐
☐
☐
☐
☐

16 Wednesday

☐
☐
☐
☐
☐
☐

OCTOBER

S	M	T	W	T	F	S
		1	2	3	4	5
6	7	8	9	10	11	12
13	14	15	16	17	18	19
20	21	22	23	24	25	26
27	28	29	30	31		

17 Thursday
○ Full Moon

18 Friday

19 Saturday

20 Sunday

October 2024

21 Monday

- [ ]
- [ ]
- [ ]
- [ ]
- [ ]
- [ ]

22 Tuesday

- [ ]
- [ ]
- [ ]
- [ ]
- [ ]
- [ ]

23 Wednesday

- [ ]
- [ ]
- [ ]
- [ ]
- [ ]
- [ ]

OCTOBER

S	M	T	W	T	F	S
		1	2	3	4	5
6	7	8	9	10	11	12
13	14	15	16	17	18	19
20	21	22	23	24	25	26
27	28	29	30	31		

24 Thursday

- [ ]
- [ ]
- [ ]
- [ ]
- [ ]
- [ ]

25 Friday

- [ ]
- [ ]
- [ ]
- [ ]
- [ ]
- [ ]

26 Saturday

- [ ]
- [ ]
- [ ]
- [ ]
- [ ]
- [ ]

27 Sunday

- [ ]
- [ ]
- [ ]
- [ ]
- [ ]
- [ ]

October 2024

28 Monday   Labour Day (New Zealand)

- [ ]
- [ ]
- [ ]
- [ ]
- [ ]
- [ ]

29 Tuesday

- [ ]
- [ ]
- [ ]
- [ ]
- [ ]
- [ ]

30 Wednesday

- [ ]
- [ ]
- [ ]
- [ ]
- [ ]
- [ ]

November

NOVEMBER

S	M	T	W	T	F	S
					1	2
3	4	5	6	7	8	9
10	11	12	13	14	15	16
17	18	19	20	21	22	23
24	25	26	27	28	29	30

31 Thursday   Halloween

- [ ]
- [ ]
- [ ]
- [ ]
- [ ]
- [ ]

1 Friday   All Saints' Day
●New Moon

- [ ]
- [ ]
- [ ]
- [ ]
- [ ]
- [ ]

2 Saturday

- [ ]
- [ ]
- [ ]
- [ ]
- [ ]
- [ ]

3 Sunday   Daylight Saving ends

- [ ]
- [ ]
- [ ]
- [ ]
- [ ]
- [ ]

November

SUNDAY	MONDAY	TUESDAY	WEDNESDAY
27	28	29	30
3 Daylight Saving ends	4	5 Election Day	6
10 Remembrance Sunday (UK)	11 Veterans Day Remembrance Day (CAN, AUS, NZ)	12	13
17	18	19	20
24	25	26	27

 2024

THURSDAY	FRIDAY	SATURDAY	NOTES
31	1	2	
	All Saints' Day ● New Moon		
7	8	9	
14	15	16	
	○ Full Moon		
21	22	23	
28	29	30	
Thanksgiving			

OCTOBER

S	M	T	W	T	F	S
		1	2	3	4	5
6	7	8	9	10	11	12
13	14	15	16	17	18	19
20	21	22	23	24	25	26
27	28	29	30	31		

DECEMBER

S	M	T	W	T	F	S
1	2	3	4	5	6	7
8	9	10	11	12	13	14
15	16	17	18	19	20	21
22	23	24	25	26	27	28
29	30	31				

November 2024

4 Monday

- [ ]
- [ ]
- [ ]
- [ ]
- [ ]
- [ ]

5 Tuesday

Election Day

- [ ]
- [ ]
- [ ]
- [ ]
- [ ]
- [ ]

6 Wednesday

- [ ]
- [ ]
- [ ]
- [ ]
- [ ]
- [ ]

NOVEMBER

S	M	T	W	T	F	S
					1	2
3	4	5	6	7	8	9
10	11	12	13	14	15	16
17	18	19	20	21	22	23
24	25	26	27	28	29	30

7 Thursday

- [ ]
- [ ]
- [ ]
- [ ]
- [ ]
- [ ]

8 Friday

- [ ]
- [ ]
- [ ]
- [ ]
- [ ]
- [ ]

9 Saturday

- [ ]
- [ ]
- [ ]
- [ ]
- [ ]
- [ ]

10 Sunday

Remembrance Sunday (UK)

- [ ]
- [ ]
- [ ]
- [ ]
- [ ]
- [ ]

November 2024

11 Monday

Veterans Day
Remembrance Day (CAN, AUS, NZ)

- [ ]
- [ ]
- [ ]
- [ ]
- [ ]
- [ ]

12 Tuesday

- [ ]
- [ ]
- [ ]
- [ ]
- [ ]
- [ ]

13 Wednesday

- [ ]
- [ ]
- [ ]
- [ ]
- [ ]
- [ ]

NOVEMBER

S	M	T	W	T	F	S
					1	2
3	4	5	6	7	8	9
10	11	12	13	14	15	16
17	18	19	20	21	22	23
24	25	26	27	28	29	30

14 Thursday

- [ ]
- [ ]
- [ ]
- [ ]
- [ ]
- [ ]

15 Friday   O Full Moon

- [ ]
- [ ]
- [ ]
- [ ]
- [ ]
- [ ]

16 Saturday

- [ ]
- [ ]
- [ ]
- [ ]
- [ ]
- [ ]

17 Sunday

- [ ]
- [ ]
- [ ]
- [ ]
- [ ]
- [ ]

November 2024

18 Monday

- [ ]
- [ ]
- [ ]
- [ ]
- [ ]
- [ ]

19 Tuesday

- [ ]
- [ ]
- [ ]
- [ ]
- [ ]
- [ ]

20 Wednesday

- [ ]
- [ ]
- [ ]
- [ ]
- [ ]
- [ ]

NOVEMBER

S	M	T	W	T	F	S
					1	2
3	4	5	6	7	8	9
10	11	12	13	14	15	16
17	18	19	20	21	22	23
24	25	26	27	28	29	30

21 Thursday

22 Friday

23 Saturday

24 Sunday

November 2024

25 Monday

☐
☐
☐
☐
☐
☐

26 Tuesday

☐
☐
☐
☐
☐
☐

27 Wednesday

☐
☐
☐
☐
☐
☐

December

DECEMBER

S	M	T	W	T	F	S
1	2	3	4	5	6	7
8	9	10	11	12	13	14
15	16	17	18	19	20	21
22	23	24	25	26	27	28
29	30	31				

28 Thursday
Thanksgiving

- [ ]
- [ ]
- [ ]
- [ ]
- [ ]
- [ ]

29 Friday

- [ ]
- [ ]
- [ ]
- [ ]
- [ ]
- [ ]

30 Saturday

- [ ]
- [ ]
- [ ]
- [ ]
- [ ]
- [ ]

1 Sunday
● New Moon

- [ ]
- [ ]
- [ ]
- [ ]
- [ ]
- [ ]

 December

SUNDAY	MONDAY	TUESDAY	WEDNESDAY
1 ● New Moon	2	3	4
8	9	10	11
15 ○ Full Moon	16	17	18
22	23	24	25 Christmas Hanukkah begins at sundown
29	30 ● New Moon	31	1

 2024

THURSDAY	FRIDAY	SATURDAY	NOTES
5	6	7	_____
			_____
			_____
			_____
		Pearl Harbor Remembrance Day	_____
12	13	14	_____
			_____
			_____
			_____
			_____
			_____
19	20	21	_____
			_____
			_____
			_____
		Winter Solstice	_____

NOVEMBER

S	M	T	W	T	F	S
					1	2
3	4	5	6	7	8	9
10	11	12	13	14	15	16
17	18	19	20	21	22	23
24	25	26	27	28	29	30

26	27	28
Boxing Day (CAN, UK, AUS, NZ) Kwanzaa begins		
2	3	4

JANUARY 2025

S	M	T	W	T	F	S
			1	2	3	4
5	6	7	8	9	10	11
12	13	14	15	16	17	18
19	20	21	22	23	24	25
26	27	28	29	30	31	

December 2024

2 Monday

3 Tuesday

4 Wednesday

DECEMBER

S	M	T	W	T	F	S
1	2	3	4	5	6	7
8	9	10	11	12	13	14
15	16	17	18	19	20	21
22	23	24	25	26	27	28
29	30	31				

5 Thursday

- [ ]
- [ ]
- [ ]
- [ ]
- [ ]
- [ ]

6 Friday

- [ ]
- [ ]
- [ ]
- [ ]
- [ ]
- [ ]

7 Saturday
Pearl Harbor
Remembrance Day

- [ ]
- [ ]
- [ ]
- [ ]
- [ ]
- [ ]

8 Sunday

- [ ]
- [ ]
- [ ]
- [ ]
- [ ]
- [ ]

December 2024

9 Monday

- [ ] _____
- [ ] _____
- [ ] _____
- [ ] _____
- [ ] _____
- [ ] _____

10 Tuesday

- [ ] _____
- [ ] _____
- [ ] _____
- [ ] _____
- [ ] _____
- [ ] _____

11 Wednesday

- [ ] _____
- [ ] _____
- [ ] _____
- [ ] _____
- [ ] _____
- [ ] _____

DECEMBER

S	M	T	W	T	F	S
1	2	3	4	5	6	7
8	9	10	11	12	13	14
15	16	17	18	19	20	21
22	23	24	25	26	27	28
29	30	31				

12 Thursday

- [ ]
- [ ]
- [ ]
- [ ]
- [ ]
- [ ]

13 Friday

- [ ]
- [ ]
- [ ]
- [ ]
- [ ]
- [ ]

14 Saturday

- [ ]
- [ ]
- [ ]
- [ ]
- [ ]
- [ ]

15 Sunday   ○ Full Moon

- [ ]
- [ ]
- [ ]
- [ ]
- [ ]
- [ ]

December 2024

16 Monday

- [ ]
- [ ]
- [ ]
- [ ]
- [ ]
- [ ]

17 Tuesday

- [ ]
- [ ]
- [ ]
- [ ]
- [ ]
- [ ]

18 Wednesday

- [ ]
- [ ]
- [ ]
- [ ]
- [ ]
- [ ]

DECEMBER

S	M	T	W	T	F	S
1	2	3	4	5	6	7
8	9	10	11	12	13	14
15	16	17	18	19	20	21
22	23	24	25	26	27	28
29	30	31				

19 Thursday

☐
☐
☐
☐
☐
☐

20 Friday

☐
☐
☐
☐
☐
☐

21 Saturday   Winter Solstice

☐
☐
☐
☐
☐
☐

22 Sunday

☐
☐
☐
☐
☐
☐

December 2024

23 Monday

- [ ]
- [ ]
- [ ]
- [ ]
- [ ]
- [ ]

24 Tuesday

- [ ]
- [ ]
- [ ]
- [ ]
- [ ]
- [ ]

25 Wednesday

Christmas
Hanukkah begins at sundown

- [ ]
- [ ]
- [ ]
- [ ]
- [ ]
- [ ]

DECEMBER

S	M	T	W	T	F	S
1	2	3	4	5	6	7
8	9	10	11	12	13	14
15	16	17	18	19	20	21
22	23	24	25	26	27	28
29	30	31				

26 Thursday

Boxing Day
(CAN, UK, AUS, NZ)

Kwanzaa begins

☐
☐
☐
☐
☐
☐

27 Friday

☐
☐
☐
☐
☐
☐

28 Saturday

☐
☐
☐
☐
☐
☐

29 Sunday

☐
☐
☐
☐
☐
☐

December 2024

30 Monday ● New Moon

- [ ]
- [ ]
- [ ]
- [ ]
- [ ]
- [ ]

31 Tuesday

- [ ]
- [ ]
- [ ]
- [ ]
- [ ]
- [ ]

1 Wednesday New Year's Day 2025

- [ ]
- [ ]
- [ ]
- [ ]
- [ ]
- [ ]

January 2025

JANUARY

S	M	T	W	T	F	S
			1	2	3	4
5	6	7	8	9	10	11
12	13	14	15	16	17	18
19	20	21	22	23	24	25
26	27	28	29	30	31	

2 Thursday

- ☐
- ☐
- ☐
- ☐
- ☐
- ☐

3 Friday

- ☐
- ☐
- ☐
- ☐
- ☐
- ☐

4 Saturday

- ☐
- ☐
- ☐
- ☐
- ☐
- ☐

5 Sunday

- ☐
- ☐
- ☐
- ☐
- ☐
- ☐

2025

JANUARY
S	M	T	W	T	F	S
			1	2	3	4
5	6	7	8	9	10	11
12	13	14	15	16	17	18
19	20	21	22	23	24	25
26	27	28	29	30	31	

FEBRUARY
S	M	T	W	T	F	S
						1
2	3	4	5	6	7	8
9	10	11	12	13	14	15
16	17	18	19	20	21	22
23	24	25	26	27	28	

MARCH
S	M	T	W	T	F	S
						1
2	3	4	5	6	7	8
9	10	11	12	13	14	15
16	17	18	19	20	21	22
23	24	25	26	27	28	29
30	31					

APRIL
S	M	T	W	T	F	S
		1	2	3	4	5
6	7	8	9	10	11	12
13	14	15	16	17	18	19
20	21	22	23	24	25	26
27	28	29	30			

MAY
S	M	T	W	T	F	S
				1	2	3
4	5	6	7	8	9	10
11	12	13	14	15	16	17
18	19	20	21	22	23	24
25	26	27	28	29	30	31

JUNE
S	M	T	W	T	F	S
1	2	3	4	5	6	7
8	9	10	11	12	13	14
15	16	17	18	19	20	21
22	23	24	25	26	27	28
29	30					

JULY
S	M	T	W	T	F	S
		1	2	3	4	5
6	7	8	9	10	11	12
13	14	15	16	17	18	19
20	21	22	23	24	25	26
27	28	29	30	31		

AUGUST
S	M	T	W	T	F	S
					1	2
3	4	5	6	7	8	9
10	11	12	13	14	15	16
17	18	19	20	21	22	23
24	25	26	27	28	29	30
31						

SEPTEMBER
S	M	T	W	T	F	S
	1	2	3	4	5	6
7	8	9	10	11	12	13
14	15	16	17	18	19	20
21	22	23	24	25	26	27
28	29	30				

OCTOBER
S	M	T	W	T	F	S
			1	2	3	4
5	6	7	8	9	10	11
12	13	14	15	16	17	18
19	20	21	22	23	24	25
26	27	28	29	30	31	

NOVEMBER
S	M	T	W	T	F	S
						1
2	3	4	5	6	7	8
9	10	11	12	13	14	15
16	17	18	19	20	21	22
23	24	25	26	27	28	29
30						

DECEMBER
S	M	T	W	T	F	S
	1	2	3	4	5	6
7	8	9	10	11	12	13
14	15	16	17	18	19	20
21	22	23	24	25	26	27
28	29	30	31			

Notes

Notes

Notes

Notes

Notes

Notes

Notes

Planners & Stationery
by Sellers Publishing, Inc.

HighNoteCollection.com